Going Out

Written by Helen Depree • Illustrated by Judith Trevelyan

I am putting on my sweater
and my jeans
and my sneakers.
I am going to play with my friend.

I am putting on my shorts
and my shoes
and my jersey.
I am going to play soccer.

I am putting on my swimsuit
and my sunglasses
and my hat.
I am going to the beach.

I am putting on my shirt
and my trousers
and my shiny shoes.
I am going to a party.

I am putting on my pajamas
and washing my face
and brushing my teeth.
I am going to bed.

11